I0481846

THE PASSIVE WRITER

5 STEPS TO EARNING MONEY IN YOUR SLEEP

Damon Brown & Jeanette Hurt

www.JoinDamon.me / www.JeanetteHurt.com

TWITTER/INSTAGRAM:

@BROWNDAMON / @BYJEANETTEHURT

CONSULTING & SPEAKING REQUESTS:

DAMON@DAMONBROWN.NET /

JHURT@SBCGLOBAL.NET

PUBLISHED BY:
Damon Brown & Jeanette Hurt

The Passive Writer
1st Edition
Copyright 2018 Damon Brown & Jeanette Hurt
Cover designed by Bec Loss

For Quinn, Alec & Abhi.
We do this for you.

The Passive Writer

SELECTED BOOKS BY THE AUTHORS

THE ULTIMATE BITE-SIZED ENTREPRENEUR:

76 WAYS TO BOOST FOCUS, TIME & PRODUCTIVITY

ON YOUR BIG IDEA

BRING YOUR WORTH:

LEVEL UP YOUR CREATIVE POWER, VALUE & SERVICE

TO THE WORLD

DRINK LIKE A WOMAN:

SHAKE. STIR. CONQUER. REPEAT.

INTRO

When 2018 began, Damon's cash flow had slowed down to a trickle. It wasn't a matter of work, as his regular column for *Inc.* was thriving, and his corporate clientele base was increasing - and had, in fact, jumped from the previous year. His coaching practice was also taking off. The challenge he faced wasn't getting the work, nor even accomplishing the work: it was the money he possessed on hand. A contract can't be cashed, nor can an invoice make a mortgage payment. He faced that strange, yet all-too-common, cyclical freelance gap when you are busy, but you are broke.

Thankfully, he still had checks coming in while he worked, when he played with his two toddlers, and even when he slept. There were the book royalties, which earned him anywhere from a couple dollars to several hundred dollars a month, from titles going back nearly a decade. More notably were his *Inc.* column, bringing in monthly residuals based on clicks, and his online bootcamp launched in mid January. Knowing a cash flow crunch was coming, Damon reached out to his community before it actually hit. He asked them how he could best serve them, and their response gave him the idea to design a self-guided online course using the basic ideas of his best-selling book, THE BITE-SIZED ENTREPRENEUR, and showing people how to put those principles into practice.

Designing this course took only a few hours a week since he already had written four books on the topic, but the impact on his income was tremendous. His "active" income checks finally started arriving in mid-to-late February, but his passive income checks kept his business humming along quite nicely. For the first six weeks of 2018, Damon lived on only the residuals from all of the work he accomplished weeks, months, and even as much as a dozen years before. Without consciously creating passive income, Damon would have had zero new cash at the start of 2018.

In early 2017, Jeanette's time was pushed to its limits. She had just launched her ninth book and first hardcover, DRINK LIKE A WOMAN, but as any writer knows, you don't stop your regular writing gigs to either write or promote a book. Not only that, but her son had just been promoted to the level of team gymnastics, and, as the primary caregiver, she found herself spending hours more in the car, traveling to practices and meets. Though she managed to sneak in interviews and write stories while her son was at practice, she increased her income mostly by making every task count and multi-purposing everything she did.

A foodie and experienced recipe developer, she used her regular recipe gigs to feed her family while earning a good wage, and she also nabbed a ghostwriting gig for a popular Canadian dietician. Since her favorite pastime has always been reading, she also reached out to a book reviewing website, and she began regularly turning her hobby into cold cash.

What we do to increase our income isn't revolutionary. But it's smart, it fits into our regular work projects, and in this book, we'll show you how you, too, can take these skills to create new streams of money. The skills you need aren't new areas of research, fresh expertise in a field, or bright ideas from something entirely different than what you do today. It is, in fact, the opposite.

In *The Passive Writer*, you will discover the fields of gold you can discover underneath the areas you've already been cultivating. Whether you realize it or not, your years in your career, and in other fields of work, have primed you perfectly to bring in residuals without breaking much of a sweat. The biggest strength we have as writers is that we highlight other people's expertise: Journalists capture one's life mission in a few paragraphs, authors build character storylines in a slim volume, and content creators inspire others to support a company's cause. This is also our weakness. We spend so much time uplifting others, going after one story, book or idea after another, and building the arguments for still others, we become accustomed to being the people behind the scenes. But what we often fail to recognize is that in researching other people's areas of expertise, we ourselves have become the experts.

This is perhaps the biggest key to passive income: Recognizing yourself not only as a beat writer, but as an expert in your field. People want to hear from you. They want to buy your services or products. They want what have to offer. All you have to do is figure out what they want the most and then organize a painless way for them to get it. Then, you just need to get out the way.

We have discovered five major tenets to creating a strong passive income:
1. Get out of one-and-done.
2. Work now to get unlimited checks later.
3. Unpackage those latent skills you take for granted.
4. Review the work you've already done.
5. Not all passive income is passive.

Notice the pattern: None of the steps require you reinvent the wheel. We both began in the newsroom where you were only as accomplished as your next story and every day when you entered was like proving yourself over again with a new slate of leads to pursue and track down. Everything was one-and-done, and even if a story did change, then it was your job to do another story updating the previous one that ran and making your own work obsolete. To put it bluntly, your work was often rendered obsolete by the time the early edition appeared the next morning. That newsroom environment has now expanded to virtually all realms of journalism and writing, and that 24 hours of relevance has been shrunk down to 24 seconds, or even less. This same discussion can be applied to magazine writers, content creators, and other creative writing fields.

Passive income isn't natural to you, then, because it requires that you embrace the opposite mentality. We have spent decades as full-time freelance journalists, and it took years for us to unlearn the pattern of becoming an expert on a story topic, then chucking out the work once the story ran and starting the process over again on the next topic, or going deep on a particular beat and using that hard earned wisdom to highlight the people being interviewed or as little jewels in the narrative itself. Those notes, those skills required to take those notes, and those insights gained along the way are of value to others.

You, first, need to recognize it yourself. And celebrate it.

-Damon Brown & Jeanette Hurt, June 2018

I
GET OUT OF ONE-AND-DONE
Repackage, repurpose & reuse your work as you work, multiplying your income exponentially

Forget the one-and-done. We get it. We're writers - we go after shiny things, and as soon as we turn in that story or book, we've already fallen in love with a totally different subject, and we've moved onto the next thing, tossing those pages (and hours) of research into the wind.

You might as well as be throwing dollar bills out of your car window as you speed down the interstate - you're losing that much money.

Before we even pitch an assignment, we are already analyzing how we can turn one simple story into multiple works - and streams of income. Jeanette is a master of interviewing, say, a bartender about her experiences, using it for her book, then turning it into three different articles for non-competing magazines and websites, and then revisiting that same person or idea a year later, and turning it into yet another assignment or two. And for every book she's written, she's more than doubled her advances in story assignments, speaking gigs, recipe development projects and private classes. "If I'm assigned a profile of an interesting person for a local magazine, my first thought is: can I write about this person for a national publication or website?" Jeanette says.

Jeanette profiled an 89-year-old bartender in her book, DRINK LIKE A WOMAN. She told this feisty woman's story in several talks she's done about the history of women and bartending, profiled her for an online magazine, and then turned around and wrote yet another profile of her for a local food magazine. Just this week, she turned one aspect of this woman's intriguing life into another online story: all she had to do is review her previous notes, skim through her already published stories, and do a quick 30-minute interview to update the story and change its slant.

Writers profile interesting people all the time. Most of the time, writers will google their subject ahead of their interview, but instead of just researching the person, research where they've been written about. Think about what national publications might be interested in this person; or, if you're interviewing someone for a national publication, what local newspapers or magazines might be interested in a quick Q & A. And remember to ask them about their alma mater - plenty of universities have well-paying alumni magazines, and you might want to pitch those, too. And while you're at it, find out the name of their hometowns: many communities, both small and large, have newspapers, magazines and online publications (that pay) for profiles. If the person is really intriguing, hang onto your notes to mine them for future spinoffs.

If you are diving deep into a subject - say, a big research paper or a book - figure out if there are smaller sidebars and quick hit stories you might be able to research at the same time. In the case of the now-92-year-old bartender, Jeanette is retelling the story of how she and her girlfriends threw their bras on the ceiling of her bar in the 1960s; her book has a cocktail honoring that act called The Bra Burner.

"My first two books were about cheese," Jeanette says. "Just last weekend, I headlined a Wisconsin cheese festival, and my speaking fee amounted to half of my first book advance, and my family enjoyed a free weekend at a resort."

Accountants will tell you that to raise your bottom line, you either have to increase your income or lower your expenses. Your expenses aren't just money, but time, energy, and focus. Time is an unreplenishable resource, as you will never get more of it once it is lost. Energy is precious because it is limited and naturally creates an opportunity cost for tomorrow; spending energy on something right now means you'll have less energy to spend on a new opportunity that may be even better.

Focus is important because, as a writer, you are often the only person organizing your schedule and, particularly if you are a freelancer, what you focus on today will quite literally change the arc of your career. Time, energy, and focus are not to be trifled with.

As for time, check in with yourself regularly to make sure you're spending it wisely. Make time for planning - and focus and energy - but doing these check-ins. Damon does this by a morning practice of meditation, using the principles of Zen Buddhism. Jeanette does this by following the Catholic contemplative method of prayer. What they both have in common is that they do their best to actually note how they are using their time - and then see if they are spending that time wisely. Damon recently went on a social media fast, and the additional time and focus helped his income rise. This inspired Jeanette (who can't completely fast from social media because her son's coaches and teachers keep in touch mostly in this fashion) to avoid Facebook and Instagram during work hours.

Energy can be managed in a few different ways and, for Damon and Jeanette, meditation and contemplation are the keys. Some people, some work projects, and some friends and family members (in both real life and social media) drain your productivity. While you can't always eliminate every single energy drain from your life, if you are aware of them, you can better deal with them, thus freeing up more energy for productive work and living.

Damon and Jeanette find that if they manage time and spend energy wisely, their focus at work becomes easier, and they accomplish more. That's not to say they don't sometimes fritter time away frivolously, waste energy on irrelevant things, and thus lose focus. But when they do their best to be cognizant of things, they not only free up more time and energy to get ongoing projects done, but it gives them the freedom and creativity necessary to develop passive streams of income.

You want to get out of the mentality of one-and-done, but that can only occur if you stop, strategize, and *then* execute. Find a centering practice that works for you - meditation, prayer, walking, journaling - so that you can see where you actually are spending your time and energy and where spending your time and energy will give you the focus to hone in on the biggest payoffs.

Thoughts to Ponder:
1. How much of your income is related to singular or one-and-done projects? If you are unsure how to calculate this, list all of your completed projects for the past month or two, then come up with a percentage?
2. Now, ask yourself: of these singular assignments and work projects, do any of them have legs? How about the rest?
3. Set aside two hours - put it down in your calendar - for a time and energy analysis. This is like reviewing your house for energy efficiencies and inefficiencies. Use these two hours to analyze where you are putting your time and energy. Be honest: what are time and energy sucks? Which of these

time and energy sucks can be just completely eliminated, and which ones simply have to be managed better?

4. Consider a social media fast, a Netflix fast, or a smartphone fast. Whatever and wherever you fritter away your time, consider fasting from the activity. If you plan a fast of any kind, set a time limit - and find at least one person to help hold you accountable.

5. Moving forward, how are you planning to better manage your projects, time and energy? And if you have any amazing insights or ideas, we'd love to hear from you (as we are always looking to improve our lives, too!).

II

WORK NOW TO GET
UNLIMITED CHECKS LATER

*Work now, then enjoy residuals from the
finished work later on*

Don't get hung up on how much you're
bringing in. Focus on how you're bringing it in.
You may have an opportunity to work a little
and have small, regular checks come in, and
those opportunities don't often shine as
brightly as the big, one-and-done money
projects. The larger, standalone business
sounds good on paper, and it feels even better
when it hits your bank account, but the lure of
the big deals can actually hurt your income.

In general, the bigger the opportunity, the
longer it will take to seal the deal and/or to get
the money. Take the traditional book industry
route: You get an agent, then you get a book
proposal in tip-top shape, then you get
publishers interested, then you negotiate the
deal, and *then* you get paid. Each of these
intervals can take more than six months and,
based on Damon and Jeanette's experiences as
well as other veteran writers, they usually take
years. It took Damon two agents and four

years to find a home for his first major book, and Jeanette toiled away at dozens of rejected book proposals for five long years before selling her first proposal.

So, the big question is: How do you feed yourself if you are totally focused and dependent on a long-term project coming through? You don't, unless you've got a plan to get money outside of the traditional systems.

While you're working away to achieve that big project, be sure to build-in smaller, related projects that can bring in income while you're still waiting for the go-ahead. The classic adage "Do not quit your day job" applies here: Damon built his first entrepreneurial pursuit, the quote-capturing app So Quotable, while still focusing on journalism income, and didn't go full throttle into entrepreneurship until his second app, Cuddlr, became a major hit two years later; Jeanette leaned on freelance writing for years as she explored public speaking, ghostwriting, and recipe development, until those alternative sources organically grew into more of her annual income. Treat them like side hustles or experiments, so the worst problem you have is juggling two different

16

income streams. Alternatively, if you leave your main source of income and bet it all on a *potential* income, then the worst case scenario is that you end up with no income.

Your financial security is far from guaranteed anyway, even if you get the proverbial brass ring of, say, a six-figure deal. Book deals are often paid out in three (or more) parts: On signing, on halfway complete manuscript, and on completely edited manuscript. A book of stature that warrants a six-figure deal usually takes years after the deal is signed. If it takes you three years to finalize a manuscript for a $100,000 deal, then you're getting $33,000 annually and, once you account for taxes and the agent's 15% - 20% cut, your payoff is looking more like $20,000 a year. You'd almost be eligible for Medicaid. And if this is your only income, if you have dependents, you might be close to qualifying for other assistance. This really isn't far-fetched, as the year Jeanette's fifth book came out, she and her family were $2 away from qualifying for such aid.

It's not knocking those big book deals, but it's important to recognize what those numbers really mean. It isn't a slam on the traditional writing business in general, nor the traditional publishing industry specifically. It is understanding the effort, time, and cash flow tied up when you put all your proverbial eggs into a system you don't control. In previous generations, your creative forefathers and foremothers were almost entirely dependent on the whims of a slow-moving, capricious system because they didn't have much of a choice. Today, you have a choice.

Right now, Jeanette is working on two different books for two different traditional publishers. While the books are exciting and fun to write, the advances are low - typical for today's publishing environment. But, they have great potential for royalties, they're in her wheelhouse, and they enable her to write stories related to the books right now, as she's researching the books, so she's decided to go ahead with the projects.

Since they aren't going to be money-makers as she's writing them, Jeanette has to earn her income the way she usually earns her income: By writing stories, testing recipes and giving speeches.

Damon's Bite-Sized Entrepreneur bootcamp is actually a passive income version of another money maker: coaching. After the first *Bite-Sized Entrepreneur* book, readers began asking him to coach them on productivity, focus, and entrepreneurship. There is only one Damon, though, and he knew there would eventually be a limitation to how much coaching he could do along with writing, consulting, and any future projects. The six-step online bootcamp captured the basics of his coaching program and funneled them into a self-guided experience. And, if people wanted a deeper dive, Damon gave bootcamp participants a package discount on one-on-one coaching. The "active" income coaching inspired the passive-income bootcamp which, in turn, helped him earn more "active" income, too. He extended the well-priced bootcamp/coaching packages to all his products - including this one under **Your Next Steps**.

Damon also began signing up people and getting paid for his bootcamp before it went live, which confirmed the interest of the people and also helped fund the time that would be spent organizing the bootcamp launch. It's possible to start your passive income *before* your product is out. Who would pay you to reach people on your upcoming or current blog? Who would write a check to sponsor your talk? Who would donate product to your class? For instance, author and Write Now writing coach Rochelle Melander adds affiliate links to her blog at http://www.writenowcoach.com. Affiliate links give you a share of any sales done on another website, like Amazon giving you a small percentage of a sale done when a visitor clicks through your website to buy something. "The challenge for me as a writer was going that extra step to both recommend products and add that affiliate link," she says. " It's not a big thing, but it does take time."

The most powerful passive income opportunities *will* take time, but we often don't take the time to do it. The more independent you are and closer you are to the freelance lifestyle, the more energy or, at minimum, anxiety is focused on courting new business, wrapping up current work, and invoicing completed works. The sacrifice can feel too great to plan for the next year's rewards, nevertheless the next quarter.

The beauty is we are actually giving space for future success. During the five years Jeanette didn't have a book deal - and it seemed like every single writer friend in her circle had a deal or had already published one, if not several books - she decided it was worth her time and energy to master the art of writing a book proposal and then mastering the art of sending said proposals out to agents and publishers. It was disappointing, frustrating, infuriating work, but with her husband's support and Damon's cheerleading, she kept at it. "I couldn't control whether my book proposals were accepted, but I could decide that I would learn how to write a great book proposal," she says. "And that became my goal: just to learn be able to write a great book proposal. I also did my best not to stay discouraged when these book proposals, which were getting better and better and easier and easier to write, were rejected."

After writing and sending out perhaps 20 different proposals, finally, Jeanette sold her first proposal. She contacted an agent who was interested in representing her to let her know she'd landed her first project - and not only did that agent take her on, but two weeks after selling her first proposal, she had a second book project land in her lap.

It probably took Jeanette six months to craft her first book proposal, but now she can write the first draft of one in less than a week. She's put in her proverbial Malcolm Gladwell 10,000 hours and then some - and by the end of next year, she'll have written and published a dozen books. "Book proposal writing and book writing are two skills that have made me very sellable as a freelance writer," Jeanette says. "Because I've written so many books, whenever I meet new editors, they're more likely to assign me stories, especially if they're related to topics I've written books on. It's definitely paid me dividends over and over again."

Mastering a new skill isn't the only way to earn more income passively. One very simple passive income technique related to doing the work now is asking for *more* money now. If someone has already reached out to you to pen a story, research a book or compile a white paper, why not ask for more? Sometimes, by just asking, you can get an extra $10, or, maybe even an extra $1,000.

When asking for more, ask politely. *Six-Figure Freelancing* author Kelly James Enger, in many of her writing classes, has writers repeat this mantra: "That sounds a little low. How about X amount?"

The worst thing a client can say is "No", but sometimes, they'll say yes. Jeanette recently asked for double what she was initially going to charge for a speaking engagement - and she tacked on mileage and expenses. "I would have been ecstatically happy with less, but I figured I know the subject really well, and the worst they would tell me is that it was out of their budget," she says. "They paid it without blinking an eye." When Jeanette is asked to speak at an event or teach a class, she automatically thinks of the contacts she's made in whatever endeavor that is, and she reaches out, via phone or email, to see if someone will sponsor the event with either a dollar or in-kind donation. That way, she doesn't have to spend money on materials for her class so her take-home pay is higher.

Author and coach Andrea King Collier recommends asking more than what you think you should make because, as creatives, we tend to underestimate our worth. Use your best judgement when it comes to asking for more, but don't be afraid of the act of asking - you can always get paid less, but maybe you'll get more.

Damon met an editor who asked him to write a piece related to some of his previous books. He simply asked "Since I'm such an expert on X, would you be comfortable paying me 25 percent more?" They were comfortable - and he increased his pay for that project as easily as if he was sleeping. Asking for more - and then getting it - really is as easy as earning money in your sleep. It simply requires being confident in your work - and your worth - and then simply asking the question.

Thoughts to Ponder:

1. What skills do you need to develop to earn more income?
2. How much time do you need to develop those skills?
3. Can you carve out a certain amount of time every week dedicated to developing those skills? Or is there a short-term class you could take to develop those skills? Are there books you could read to help you further your expertise? Is there a coach you could hire to help you develop these skills?
4. Where do you need to make more time to create a better life for yourself? How can you build this time into your life?
5. Who can you ask for more money, right now?

III

PACKAGE THOSE LATENT SKILLS
YOU TAKE FOR GRANTED

Where do people find value in you? What are some of your unique skills and talents? Discover ways to earn money from your latent talents and learn how to package those skills for others

Forget the one-and-done. We get it. We're writers - we go after shiny things, and as soon as we turn in that story or book, we've already fallen in love with a totally different subject, and we've moved onto the next thing, tossing those pages (and hours) of research into the wind.

Jeanette holds a theory that everyone has a superpower or sometimes even two or more, and you can either use these innate skills for good like a superhero, or you can use them for evil, like a supervillain. One of her superpowers - which she perfected in boring Mrs. Rakebrand's fifth grade homeroom - is speed reading. Jeanette uses it regularly to research her books and articles, but mostly, she just uses it for enjoyment, as she typically reads about a dozen books a week.

After a conversation with her son, Quinn, whose superpower is energy (related to gymnastics, breaking windows, and climbing roofs), she realized that maybe she should be using her superpower as a source of income. A posting on the American Society of Journalists and Authors job board sought book reviewers so, even though she had a crazy busy week, she popped out a quick, introductory email, and she got the gig. Now, at least two or three of the books she would be reading for fun, she's reading for profit - and it's not cutting into her busy life.

As a food and beverage writer, Jeanette also loves playing around in the kitchen or behind her home bar. When she cooks dinner and tries out new recipes, she makes a note of which recipes could be adapted and used for her recipe development clients. But the first four years of her freelancing career, she didn't develop a single recipe for publication. She took cooking classes, interviewed chefs and restaurateurs, and wrote plenty of food and beverage stories, but she doubted her own knowledge base and skills to develop recipes, never mind that she regularly developed recipes for her family and friends to enjoy.

"When I first started freelancing, I thought most recipe developers had to have a more formal cooking or cheffing background," she says. "Once I realized many recipe developers were writers just like me - people who had great palates and enthusiasm for home cooking - I realized that maybe, I, too, could do this for money."

Armed with *The Recipe Writer's Handbook* by Barbara Gibbs Ostmann and Jane L. Baker, she gathered the courage to pitch herself as a recipe developer. Slowly, she gained one client, and then another, and she's been writing recipes for magazines, websites, and books ever since.

Jeanette made a common freelancing mistake - not recognizing that she already possessed skills and talents other people would pay her to use.

What skills and knowledge base do you have? And don't just look at the stories and "expertise" in your written world - what do you do in your everyday life and do really well? Are you a financial writer who runs the concession stands at your daughter's soccer tournament? Do you craft homemade gifts around the holidays? Do you throw awesome tiki parties? Do you watch every crime show known to man? Are you an expert at removing unidentifiable laundry stains? Did you go through something really challenging and difficult and come out the other side stronger?

All of your life experiences can be mined for stories, projects, essays, books, and more. Learn to recognize that you are an expert in all the things you probably take for granted. Don't assume that because a task is easy for you, it's easy for everyone else. Don't assume everyone has the same knowledge base or skill set as you, and don't assume that you are lacking in a knowledge base or skill set.

Damon managed to balance running a startup, speaking engagements at TED and other major conferences, all the while continuing to write books and articles. At the same time, he became the primary caretaker of his two young sons. Despite the balancing act, his main professional focus was still on covering tech culture. However, at events, online, and in passing, people began asking him what seemed to be an odd question: "How do you do it all?" Damon assumed that everyone juggled everything, because, to him, that's just what you do, but this persistent question, which kept coming up over and over again, made him realize that it wasn't normal and, perhaps, he had a certain insight that other equally ambitious primary caretakers did not.

What happened was a pivot: Damon moved from simply discussing the power of tech to how tech can help you balance your life to how you can follow your most exciting ideas within the context of your current life. Tech, by itself, went to the wayside. The shift went full throttle with his book *The Bite-Sized Entrepreneur: 21 Ways to Ignite Your Passion & Pursue Your Side Hustle,* which hit the Amazon Top 10 Entrepreneurship books. The popularity of the book led to speaking about productivity, focus, and balance, and to an even more intimate discussion with one-on-one coaching. An online boot-camp based on *The Bite-Sized Entrepreneur* series, now a trilogy, became popular, too, and was an avatar in his passive income pursuit: A self-guided experience that Damon invested time and energy into in to launch to provide him passive residuals later. It all came from listening to what people were asking of him.

Thoughts to Ponder:
1. What do you do, everyday, that you aren't paid for? Really, think about this, and perhaps, set aside some time to journal, pray or ponder this question.
2. What are your superpowers?
3. What do you love, outside of writing and relationships, more than anything else in the world? If you're not writing about it, why not?
4. Are there any intersections between questions one through three?
5. Can you turn something you do anyway, something you love anyway, and/or something you're really good at anyway, into a stream of income?

IV
REVIEW THE WORK YOU'VE ALREADY DONE

Old material can become today's new money. Discover ways of analyzing past work for future income

If you're concentrating all of your efforts on creating a one of a kind, bespoke experiences for individual customers, you're not only wasting some of your time, but you're also not necessarily best serving those customers. Simply put: If all of your work is one-of-a-kind, then you're missing out.

We're not talking about replacing such custom work with a generic substitute that you slap together and just push onto your clients. Instead, we want to encourage you to go deeper. Do some upfront work - do the research, examine the feedback loop, and complete the legwork - to understand what your customers need the most, then figure out what they all have in common, and finally, create a universal experience to feed them on as many levels as possible.

One problem is that many of us feel guilty when we don't customize everything for each customer. Here's a brief example: Damon wrote *The Bite-Sized Entrepreneur*, which became a best-seller, so he expanded it into a trilogy. He was asked to speak about the topics presented in those books, and that, in turn, created media appearances, college and corporate talks, and conference stages. After several speeches, audience members went up to Damon, asking for coaching and that started his one-on-one calls. Most recently, his audience asked him for more insight, but didn't want to commit to a coaching schedule, so he created a self-guided bootcamp. All were based on the same seed of information: The original *Bite-Sized Entrepreneur* book.

"Both the books and the bootcamps provide income even when I'm not working," Damon says.

Most freelancers we know are trying their very best to financially scale their business. The problem is that you doing the work isn't scalable. There is only one you. Small business owners often have the same dilemma, which is why we are often the worst bottleneck in our own system. Why? Most of us became independent creators or business owners because we love doing the work. To have more security, though, you have to give up some of the work. You have to fall more in love with serving your audience in all of the ways they need to be served - not just in one, particular way of serving them.

A simple yet very effective technique to grow your passive income is to look back at your notes, your records, and your finished projects. Though it will probably give you an ego boost to look at your successes - especially the ones you haven't thought about in a while - that's not the primary purpose of this task.

You are mining for past gems that could be shined up for new - but not difficult - projects. After our very first talk about Passive Income for Writers at the 2018 American Society of Journalists and Authors conference in New York City, a woman who specializes in writing about pets approached Jeanette.

"I want to thank you for your suggestion about repitching past stories," she says. "I never thought about doing that."

This very successful writer had an introductory meeting with an editor of a pet magazine, and our talk reminded her of one of her past successes: Two years ago, she wrote a lovely newspaper article about the extravagant ways people remodel and design homes to pamper their pets. "I pitched a new version of that story, and it looks like I might receive an assignment," she says.

Now, she can't turn in the exact same story she wrote for this national newspaper for a specialty dog magazine, but she already has identified the trends, she already has a list of sources, and she even has organized a few interesting anecdotes. All she has to do is dust off her old story and notes, then make a few phone calls to update the information, and she's got a story that she can almost write in her sleep. She already knows the information because she's sorted it out, sourced out her research, and has the general gist of what needs to be told - all she has to do is reformat the information to suit the new publication.

One of the challenges - and joys - of being a writer is getting a project on a totally new subject, researching the heck out of it, then assembling your thoughts and information to present a cohesive and coherent story or book on the subject. Along the way, you become an expert on intimacy and technology, cooking for your dog, health care legislation, best business practices for financial planners...and virtually every subject under the sun.

A strength most writers bring to the table is that unique ability to dig out, source, and then pull together information in new and interesting ways for an audience. But instead of always searching out new topics to write about, why not figure out new audiences who hunger for the same information? It's infinitely easier to write another story on a subject you've already researched and written about than to start from scratch. This whole technique is based on re-using topics you are already an expert in.

At the time of this writing, Jeanette currently has nine projects, plus two book projects, listed on her to-do list. Except for one project writing listacles for a travel website, all the rest are related to past projects (including both books!). One is a book review on a diet plan - she's written dozens of healthy recipes and interviewed too many dieticians to count so it wasn't totally new subject matter even though she'd never read a German fad diet book. Another is on non-alcoholic drinks, and she's already written six different stories on the subject, and she's also including a chapter on this in one of her books. Another is based on a woman she profiled in *Drink Like a Woman*, and still another is on a trendy cocktail she's written one previous story about. Still another is on visiting Door County to tour wineries (she's written at least half a dozen travel stories on Door County). And yet another is a recipe inspired by an editing project that should be quite easy to develop because she tested a similar recipe last year.

If you've written a personal essay on something, can you turn it into a listicle? If you've written a fact-based, heavy-interview focused feature, can you turn it into a long-form essay? If you've written several stories on a similar subject, is there something about that subject - even just one angle - that you could turn into yet another project? Or how about turning it into a book? Have you written something locally that could be refitted to a national publication or vice versa?

If you are a fiction writer, perhaps you could write a novella, a short story, or a compilation of short stories that you could self-publish? Or perhaps, you could create a fan-related event for your book and other writers' books? You might also be able to create an online course or coaching for unpublished writers in your genre. Think outside of the box of what you're already doing, but make sure it's related to work you've already done and done well.

While Jeanette still has to make phone calls to get the most-up-to-date information for these projects, she already knows who to go for to get that information. She doesn't have to spend 30 minutes on Google or calling industry experts to track down sources. "Whenever I meet a new-to-me editor, I immediately think of past stories that could be tweaked to fit a different audience," Jeanette says. "I've used this skill so many times, I almost do it automatically. It also serves me well when editors approach me and say 'I'm looking for X,' and usually I'll have Y and Z to add to their request."

One of the big challenges of being a successful writer is having so much work it's hard to juggle. "It's not just making deadlines and doing a good job on these projects - but it's also the mental energy of tackling new subject matter," Jeanette says.

Reusing your own work raises the question of plagiarizing yourself. Don't reuse quotes in stories, nor reuse actual sentences or phrases, but it is safe to reuse sources and write about some of the same subjects. Also, if a publication buys all rights, you can still write about the same subject - by using different sources, focusing on a different angle, and of course, using different quotes. And if you've written six or eight or more stories on a given subject, you also should ask yourself if maybe, just maybe there might be a book project that's related.

Beyond writing, you should also look at other ways you could make money by sharing your knowledge. Three out of the first four books Jeanette penned were about cheese. Every year, she ends up writing at least one story about cheese, and she usually ends up speaking (for money) at at least one event about cheese.

She's even combined her expertise of cheese and cocktails to create unique experiences for different customers.

"My cheese books were used to develop questions on the American Cheese Society's Cheese Professional certification exam," Jeanette says. "I know cheese really well so I now speak at different foodie events, and I teach pairing classes. It's a fun way to share information about a subject I'm passionate about."

It's about thinking creatively about subjects you know and figuring out who hungers for that information and what's the best way to get that information to those people. Sometimes, that means assembling a new article on an old subject, and sometimes, that's putting together a radio essay, and sometimes, it's consulting for someone who values your knowledge.

Thoughts to Ponder:

1. Without too much thinking, what are five projects you completed within the last five years that you loved working on?

2. Can you re-use part of any of these projects, use any of them as launchpads for new endeavors, or turn any of these ideas into bigger or smaller projects?

3. Set a timer for 10 minutes. Start listing every project you worked on in the past year. After the timer buzzes, set it again for 20 minutes. Look at your list, and analyze it. Can you mine any of these projects for other spin-offs?

4. Do you keep lists, journals or planners in which you set goals or come up with ideas? Take a trip down memory lane and revisit these lists. Are there any of these ideas that you haven't pursued that are still worth pursuing?

5. Set one actionable goal to pursue a new project that's related to an old one.

V

PASSIVE INCOME ISN'T ALWAYS PASSIVE

*Weigh the maintenance, time & focus
necessary to maintain a potential income
stream, as well as how to integrate the passive
income into your everyday earnings*

One of the biggest scams today is paying to be an overnight success: "Give me X amount of dollars, and I can make your first book an Amazon bestseller, increase your profit margins by ten times, or build your social media following to the stratosphere." This promise of the world on a platter is as old as time, but the web has seemingly multiplied your odds of hitting it big, and even any real advantages from our connected world seem even larger than they really are. The quick path to wealth is now even more tempting, and passive income is the flavor du jour. Create, sit back, and retire early. And if you believe that, well, we have a bridge we could sell you, too.

We both will be the first to tell you that not all passive income is passive. Jeanette, through her reselling and repackaging of her interviews, and Damon, with his multiple products and services from the same source, evaluate each and every new thing they create. Let's be clear: Even freelance writing, where you have a set demand, you create the product, and then you receive payment for said product, is relatively structured compared to passive income streams. You know how it works. But with passive income, this requires creating paths of income, often completely on your own. That means you don't know the truth about how many people will buy it (so you can't easily determine how much you'll actually make), you don't know what time you should launch this new thing, as there is often no external deadlines like lead times or closing dates, and it's often unclear from the outset how you're going to get it to the purchaser until you're well into the process. Paying someone who is guaranteeing you six-figure passive income streams when you haven't established any passive income streams already is a fool's errand.

Passive income is a risk of resources, often of time, money, or both. Do not believe anyone who tells you otherwise. In the same spirit, the most dangerous thing you can think is, "This is passive income, so it must be good!" Not all passive incomes are created equal.

Your passive income should be evaluated based on three factors: Potential consistency, expected work, and ease of launch. Potential consistency is how often you expect people to pay for your work. Expected work is how much effort you have to put into creating it. Ease of launch is the energy required to get it out the door. Let's dive into the three levels.

Potential consistency is asking, "Do people actually want this?" *Actually* is the most important word here, as writers, like many creators, have a skewed view of what others need. We get up, brush our teeth and shower (hopefully), do our morning ritual, and, eventually, sit in solitude for hours on end. Your routine may be the coffee shop or the cubicle, or it could be sunrise or in the midnight hour. Writing - creating - is almost always a solitary activity, and many of us are driven to talk about something, are assigned to research it, and, no matter through a romantic travel expedition in the Andes, deep dive into the local library, or copious interviews with subject-matter experts, it all comes down to us sitting by ourselves and making something. It is a one-way street. Passive income requires the opposite intention: Understanding your ideal consumers' needs by building a conversation.

Damon and Jeanette are just old enough to remember the classic newsrooms of yore, where you'd write a story, it would run, and then, days later, you'd get letters to the editor, *real* letters to the editor in the mail. Eventually, those letters turned into emails and then evolved into short-range messaging like Twitter and wall posting like Facebook. This may make you think you are more connected to your audience than the newspapers of the past, which is arguable, but that doesn't necessarily mean you know what that audience needs any more than we did in those dusty newsrooms, and, what's worse, social media can give you a false positive for what is worth your time and effort. It's frustrating to create something that gets a ton of "buzz" online and then have it fall flat in sales. A Like does not equal a sale in hand, just as much as an invoice does not equal having a check to cash.

The conversation, then, should be as intimate as possible and should begin before you try to do your resell, new product, or big launch. Your conversation could be an email newsletter, which Damon has had considerable success with recently. Your conversation could be through conferences, workshops, or meetups. Your conversation could be at coffee shops or lunches with people interested in your ideas. One simple example of this is how Damon and Jeanette network. Neither of them live in New York City, but they regularly head to town for the annual American Society of Journalists and Authors conference, a TED event, or for a book signing, they each build in additional meetings with editors, agents and even customers. Time after time, the Manhattanites not only were happy to see them, but were shocked that an out-of-town writer wanted taking time out of their schedule to connect. "You'd be surprised," they still say to this day, "almost no out-of-town writers see us." So when Jeanette pitches a resale of an interview with a food legend, or when Damon tells a New York colleague that he's got a spot open in his coaching calendar, everyone already knows what the other person does, what they need, and how the pieces fit together. The result is often a sale.

All this requires is reaching out, being open, and listening well. Recently, Jeanette was teaching a cocktail making class out-of-town, and she ran into a woman who attended one of her previous classes. This woman is now an owner of a new beverage-related business, and their simple, catch-up conversation led to Jeanette being hired to headline a special dinner. "It's asking people what they need, and if they have a need I can fill, I do so immediately," Jeanette says.

Expected work is asking, "How hard will this be to pull off?" Your passive income stream will be work, but it should be proportional to the potential long-term payoff, as well as the resources you have on hand. Be realistic about what you can accomplish with what you have going on right now. Damon, Jeanette, and other passive income writers are juggling family obligations, authoring books, full-time freelance writing, consulting, and editing, and other parts of their personal and business life.

There have been interesting, exciting projects and ideas all of us have wanted to pursue, but they didn't fit into time, energy, or schedule of our other priorities. Know when to say no. Anytime you say yes to something, you are potentially saying no to other things in the future. Ironically, getting your passive income streams started will actually give you the opportunity for more freedom to pursue other, interesting career paths!

There are a few ways to navigate the need-time-to-make-time catch 22: Push yourself beyond your limit for a short period of time to make your passive income stream real; take on incremental pieces of the idea, step by step, until you make it real; or to table it until you have more time, energy, or space. The last option is by far the most dangerous as, to paraphrase Seth Godin, we fool ourselves when we believe pursuing something will be easier tomorrow and, in most cases, it will be even harder than today.

When Damon became an entrepreneur, he jumped into the first approach, getting up at 3:15 every morning and working for three hours before his infant woke up to get his first solopreneur business, So Quotable, off the ground, and, after teetering on burnout, shifted to the second approach, making incremental progress, day by day, while managing his self care better. The first business led to him co-founding his second business, Cuddlr, which became popular enough to be acquired a year after the app launched. In the first instance, he pushed himself for nearly a year to get it done. In the second instance, he eased into a regular, persistent schedule, that gave him the stamina to lead one of the top Apple apps of 2014.

And there is a third instance, too, as both he and Jeanette have many projects, including some collaborations, that have not seen the light of day because of current circumstances, higher commitments, and bigger priorities. You have to know what is important to you and your audience, what resources you are willing and able to give, and what you will give up in the interim. The last point is key: How much time do you think you need to get this thing off the ground and what are you trading in to do it? Money? More time? Sleep? Opportunity cost of something else you could be doing? Damon gave himself a year of the crazy schedule, which created a set finish line and perhaps even prevented a bigger burnout. How much time do you need? Establish that right now.

Writers like Kelly K. James, author of *Six-Figure Freelancing*, maximize their income not just based on the rates they negotiate, but on minimizing the resources required to sell it. If you are pitching a second article based on someone you interviewed already, then it may just be a matter of using a different part of an extended interview and framing your new piece around it, which means, as emphasized earlier, there needs to be a strategy *before* you conduct the interview itself. Damon had the opportunity to interview workplace psychologist and popular TED speaker Adam Grant, and, based on the seven or so questions he asked, he was able to share Grant's insights in his *Inc. Magazine* column, another smaller column he writes, and will likely use it in one of his future books.

Is this passive pursuit, after you've evaluated it, turning into a midnight monster of an idea that's going to take more effort and time than it's really worth? Keep in mind that a good passive income source may not actually create the best passive income directly. Damon has many writing opportunities paying more than his *Inc Magazine* column, and yet the column itself puts him in front of millions of people purchasing his books and joining his bootcamp. The small passive income source feeds the bigger passive income sources, making the small one much, much bigger.

Lastly, ease of launch is asking, "What would be required to get this to the right people?" Evaluate your network of sources, clients, editors, family and friends. Who do you know who needs your project? Who do you know who might know someone who needs your expertise?

Sometimes, you have to go outside your circle of regular acquaintances, friends, family and work - and reach out to a person you only know in passing. In *The Defining Decade: Why Your Twenties Matter and How to Make the Most of Them*, clinical psychologist Meg Jay talks about going beyond your social circle to network. She describes how she once was delivered a box of books that weren't meant for her, and through getting them returned to the right person, she met the author. When she decided to write a book, she realized she didn't know any agents - but she knew this one author. This author introduced her to an agent, and she sold her book. Sometimes, it's these "six degrees of separation" or "six degrees of Kevin Bacon" kind of networking that can get you in touch with the people who need your services. But you have to be willing to reach out to people whom you might not know really well, if at all. To paraphrase what Jay discusses in her book, if someone who needed your services was in your social network, they'd already be your clients.

And even after you determine that people want it, the idea is doable, and you can execute it, then there is absolutely no guarantee of success. The best route to success is to actually assume most of your attempts will yield little to no direct rewards. Damon, Jeanette, and many other veterans have poured their energy into all of their books equally, and yet only a fraction do well enough to give royalty checks later. Imagine the frustration if you were to assume that a book were to be a financial windfall and it flops? Any passive income you pursue has to be done with a higher strategy in mind, like raising the cultural discussion or building your skill set in an area or serving a particular community. Otherwise, you risk burning out or giving up at the first time a passive income pursuit doesn't go as planned.

Instead, start small: Once a month, ask for more money than what is offered for an assignment; or pick your simplest passive income idea and spend an hour a week cultivating it; or talk to someone you trust who loves your writing and ask them how else they would like to receive you. These acts become doable, definitive steps towards you recognizing great passive income opportunities.

Thoughts to Ponder:
1. After reading all of these chapters, what is the one passive income idea you'd like to implement right now?
2. Is this idea something customers really will pay you for delivering it? Do they really need it? Is there a way for you to test it out to see if there actually is a need?
3. If there's one idea you want to pursue, would it be best implemented by talking to another person or expert? Is that person or expert within your circle, or do you need to reach out?
4. How much time does this idea take to implement?
5. Do you have that much time to spare, right now?
6. How much are you willing to sacrifice for this? Is it worth it to you, or do you need to shelve it for the time being?

SUCCESS STORIES FROM THE TRENCHES
Interviews with Passive Income overachievers

Rochelle Melander is a certified professional writing coach, speaker, and the bestselling author of ten traditionally published books, including *Write-A-Thon: Write Your Book in 26 Days (and Live to Tell About It)*. She offers tools and tips at her website, www.writenowcoach.com, and you can follow her on Twitter @WriteNowCoach.

There are different ways to look at passive income. How do you define it in your career?

Two ways. One is the do it once, earn over time model. That's how I earn money from the advertising I host on my site. That is purely passive income. Once the ad widget is installed, I do nothing more. (Except collect checks!) The second model requires a little more work. I create products—usually books and courses—and then sell them online or on my site. Although I only create the product once, these do require some additional work to keep earning money. For example, I need to plan and manage a recurring marketing cycle for each book and course.

When did you first discover that you could do something once and continue to get checks over time?

As a professional coach, I've been aware of this for years. My colleagues in the coaching world are very savvy about this. It's taken me some time to implement this in my own business.

Is there anything or anyone who inspired you to earn income passively?

I'm inspired by the world of bloggers and YouTube hosts who make money from creating fun content. Recently, I've been following a lot of people who blog about art, bullet journaling, and other paper crafts. Every time I check out one of their videos, they've discovered a new way to earn income from their blogs. It's a great place to learn about how to earn income passively.

What was your first successful attempt at passive income?

My first successful attempt at passive income was the easiest: using affiliate links in my blog posts. I didn't make a lot of money—I still don't—but I like the idea of earning income for the books and products I recommend. The challenge for me as a writer was going that extra step to both recommend products and add that affiliate link. It's not a big thing—but it does take time.

Many writers we know want to create passive income streams, but don't know how to make the leap. What is the first step you'd recommend?

I work with a lot of clients who want to write ebooks or lead courses. We always start by assessing what content they have already created that could be transformed into a book or course. For example, maybe you have been blogging for years and have a file filled with articles on finance or food. Or, you've written dozens of articles for other blogs on productivity. How could you collect these pieces into a book or course that could earn you income?

What percentage of your income is passive?
Probably about 10 percent.

What is your favorite way to earn money passively?
From books. I love writing books, and I'm always honored when someone chooses to spend their time with my information. My new venture is to offer more workshops and then to transfer them into evergreen products on my website. It's an easy way for people to learn from me, and it offers an opportunity for me to spend my time creating new products. I can help more people this way, which is great for me!

What is the most surprising source of your passive income?
Affiliate marketing. I've just started marketing courses for other writing teachers, and I earn part of what they sell from my links. It's a win-win situation. I get to promote courses I believe in, and I earn income while doing it.

What are the most overlooked sources of passive income for writers?

Affiliate marketing. We all think about creating and selling our own courses, but what about selling other people's courses and simply picking up the check?

What is the one thing writers new to passive income should know?

Passive income takes time. Visioning, planning, and management are all a part of the process. Start with a vision of how you want to earn income passively. Then create a plan for development, implementation, and marketing. Once that's in place, set aside time each week or month to manage your passive income streams. This will help you maximize the income you earn from these sources.

Andrea King Collier is a freelance multimedia journalist and essayist, and is the author of *Still With Me.. A Daughter's Journey of Love and Loss* and *The Black Woman's guide to Black Men's Health*. She coaches freelance sustainability and smart resales through a popular online course called gridding, and you can follow her on Twitter @andreacollier.

When did you first discover that you could do something once and continue to get checks over time?
When I first started teaching--eight years ago. But I added to that when I moved to create content beyond what I teach.

Is there anything or anyone who inspired you to earn income passively?
Marie Forleo. I took her class, and it wasn't so much what I learned but what I learned about how she set up passive income. She has a genius model for herself and the numbers are staggering. The novelist James Patterson also has an amazing model.

What was your first successful attempt at passive income?

Beyond my class, it was the coursepack for gridding. It was a test that I passed.

Many writers we know want to create passive income streams, but don't know how to make the leap. What is the first step you'd recommend?

Take an inventory of what you know and do well. What is that one thing that you could write or tape that people need to make their own business run smoother. Then start working on that. People think it has to be big. But it doesn't.

What percentage of your income is passive?

It varies. Right now, because I am not teaching, it is about 10 percent.

What is your favorite way to earn money passively?

I am still trying to discover it.

What is the most surprising source of your passive income?

Taking speeches and turning them into content.

What are the most overlooked sources of passive income for writers?

Resales.

What is the one thing writers new to passive income should know?

The sky's the limit, but you also have to keep building the platform for it.

Kelly K. James is a long-time freelance journalist and ghostwriter, and author of *Six-Figure Freelancing, Second Edition: The Writer's Guide to Making More Money*. You can follow her on Twitter @kellyjamesenger.

There are different ways to look at passive income. How do you define it in your career?
I look at it as "free money," or money that comes to me without me having to work (or do much work) for it. In the past, when I was doing a lot of magazine work, it was selling reprints of work to a variety of smaller and regional markets. I also produced a number of short ebooks on freelancing.Today, it's royalties—money that's already been made but that comes in without me doing any extra work.

When did you first discover that you could do something once and continue to get checks over time?

Fairly early on, I realized that if I retained reprint rights to work, I could resell them to other markets. The reprint markets were often smaller magazines or regional pubs that needed articles but were willing to buy reprinted work. For example, I sold a bunch of bridal pieces to regional bridal markets throughout the country. I made between $7,000 and $11,000 a year doing this for quite a while.

Different story: several years ago, I decided to publish a series of short books on freelancing (I also have traditionally and self-published books on freelancing). The idea was to make a little money off of them and hopefully spur some book sales. Once those were up, I promoted them on my blog (which I let lapse several years ago) and made maybe $50-100 in a typical month. Today that number is more like $25/month but I don't promote them anymore as I've gotten out of the "freelancing expert" platform.

Many writers we know want to create passive income streams, but don't know how to make the leap. What is the first step you'd recommend?

Think about what you already have on your hard drive and how you can repurpose it. Reprints are a great example of this. Writing the ebooks took little time, and they sold decently for a while. I haven't been promoting them, though, so sales are fairly insignificant now.

What percentage of your income is passive?

Not much these days. As contracts have gotten grabbier, it's been more difficult to negotiate retaining reprint rights. And today, the majority of my work is ghostwriting books and doing content for content agencies, and by its nature, that work isn't reprintable. I'd say maybe 5 percent (and that includes royalties and ebook sales). I'm hoping that my royalty checks will increase as I do more projects with back end deals, as I expand on next.

What is your favorite way to earn money passively?

Royalty checks. Some of my ghosting projects are flat-fee, but I'm now focusing on projects where I get a percentage or have some back-end provision so that if the book does well, I'll get a (typically small) portion of those proceeds.

What is the most surprising source of your passive income?

I don't think any are surprising.

What are the most overlooked sources of passive income for writers?

Repurposing what they have into something else salable, like with ebooks.

What is the one thing writers new to passive income should know?

Money you don't have to work for is more fun that money you worked for.

Jeanette's Thoughts on Passive Income

There are different ways to look at passive income. How do you define it in your career?
Anything I don't start from scratch, anything I don't have to waste time or energy to write or do extra research, is passive.

When did you first discover that you could do something once and continue to get checks over time?
When the Boy Scouts paid me a small dividend check because I wrote two small stories for their magazine at the end of the year.

Is there anything or anyone who inspired you to earn income passively?
Everyone we interviewed for this book inspires me as a writer and as a writer earning passive income.

What was your first successful attempt at passive income?
The first time I resold a local piece to a national magazine.

Many writers we know want to create passive income streams, but don't know how to make the leap. What is the first step you'd recommend?

Look over your past projects and past successes. Really identify your superpower, and put it to work earning you money.

What percentage of your income is passive?

It is really hard to quantify, in exact numbers. I would say, at least one-fifth to one-third of my income could be considered one-offs initially, but I'm always thinking of how I can reuse it so sometimes, what starts out as a one-off becomes an idea that generates thousands of dollars. Most of what I write is in my wheelhouse so just about everything I do is related. Also, whenever I get a new assignment, one of my first thoughts is can I resell this project to a non-competing publication? I recently did an interview of a big-wig in the culinary realm for a business to business publication. After it runs - and after my first piece for a different publication is accepted - I'm going to pitch him as a story. So, in a sense, a lot of what I do, gets recycled and reused in different ways.

What is your favorite way to earn money passively?

Asking for more money and then getting it.

What is the most surprising source of your passive income?

Speaking engagements.

What are the most overlooked sources of passive income for writers?

Their ideas. Writers are specialists in ideas, and we don't sell them, reuse them or market them to our best financial benefits. We also are usually our worst critics so we don't realize or recognize the skills and talents others would pay us to use - nor even simply recognize them as skills that others don't possess. I assumed most writers are speed readers, and while many writers might be speed readers, not all of them are, and most certainly, not all of them are using this skill to benefit themselves financially.

What is the one thing writers new to passive income should know?

Writing is a business. Writing takes energy and time, and to be successful, you need to use those things well. You also need to think of yourself as a business person, and you need to think of yourself as someone who deserves to be paid well for your services.

Surround yourself with positive people, and stop yourself from complaining that writers don't earn enough money for their work - whether this is true or not is beside the point. Negativity begets more negativity. Just stop yourself from complaining if you are complaining - especially online or in public.

My husband, my family and my friends are supportive of my work, and at times, they have believed in me as a writer when I lacked faith in myself. But it's also important to have at least one writer friend who writes about subject matter you don't write about to hold you accountable. Damon and I are writing goal buddies. We have both stepped in to edit each other's work before we turned it in, connected each other with publishers and agents, and boosted each other when the writing life became challenging.   Our friendship has evolved organically, but get out there and go to writing conferences, events, and signings - network, help other writers, and connect. Eventually, you, too, will find a writing friend who could help you stay on track to reach your writing goals.

Damon's Thoughts on Passive Income

There are different ways to look at passive income. How do you define it in your career?
Passive income is creating something once and getting residuals from it in the future with little or no additional effort.

When did you first discover that you could do something once and continue to get checks over time?
Books! It was early in my career, when I thought my long magazine features on the history of video games could work as one book, that I realized I was only getting paid once for all my hard work. Very few magazines at the time, and less today, actually give you a percentage when your articles are reprinted, published in anthologies, and so on. I was spending months on an article for a single check. A book, though, was a lot more work for potentially infinite pay. Still I remember that exact moment of clarity, sitting alone in my Chicago studio apartment and saying "Why didn't anyone tell me this!?" It took a few more years to publish my first major book, and the books after became a steady stream of income, even today.

Is there anything or anyone who inspired you to earn income passively?

It wasn't a hot discussion when I started full-time freelancing in 2000. My revelation was in 2003, and it was something I discovered on my own. Unfortunately, the great freelancers I knew were focused on getting in bigger pubs and pay per word, not the more entrepreneurial or long-term strategies. Kelly K. James was one of the first freelancers I met later that really discussed it.

What was your first successful attempt at passive income?

My first self-published book, *Damon Brown's Simple Guide to the iPad* in 2010. I was living in Silicon Valley at the time and heard the rumor of the iPad well before it was announced. Traditional publishers were interested in me doing a book on it, but they didn't see how they could quickly publish a book in time for the iPad launch. The Amazon Kindle was just becoming mainstream and, after talking with some of my mentors, I planned to do the book on my own: Having my dad, artist David G. Brown, create the cover, my good writer friend (and now co-author!) Jeanette do the editing, and leveraging my tech journalism contacts to get the word out. A friend and I then stayed up all night in line to be the first people in San Francisco to get an iPad, then I spent the next three days learning the ins and outs of the device. *Damon Brown's Simple Guide to the iPad* was out exactly a week after the device launched. I initially sold it for $.99 - the same price as an Apple app. Within a couple days it became the #1 book on Amazon's Tech Bestseller list and stayed on the list for nearly a year. It took months for traditional publishers to do competing books, and, by then, I was able to pay my San Francisco rent on sales of the book alone.

The passive income idea recessed into the background for a few years until I self-published *The Bite-Sized Entrepreneur: 21 Ways to Ignite Your Passion & Pursue Your SIde Hustle,* based on my adventures launching and selling a successful startup while taking care of my first infant. It also became a best-seller, hitting the Amazon Top 10 Entrepreneurship books and launching a trilogy of books and my online *Bite-Sized Entrepreneur* bootcamp. As of this month, I have a dozen and a half to two dozen passive income streams compared to just a handful three years ago.

Many writers we know want to create passive income streams, but don't know how to make the leap. What is the first step you'd recommend?
Think about what questions people ask you the most, then find a way to make it easier for people to get it. I was a journalist covering tech culture, but people would ask me for tips on the latest technology, so I created a book explaining the newest tech at the time, the iPad. I was an entrepreneur who successfully founded and sold a startup, but I was repeatedly asked how I managed to do it while being a stay-at-home dad to a baby, so I made products that showed others how to create their best creative career within their current busy lives.

What percentage of your income is passive?
For the first half of 2017, it was 10 percent. For the first two months of 2018, though, it was 100 percent. The income came strictly from my previously-published books, my bootcamp, my affiliate links, and my *Inc. Magazine* column residuals. It was an amazing, breathtaking beginning to the year.

My intention is to have 75 percent passive income to create a solid six-figure salary, making any new projects I pursue more optional than necessary. It also shifts my focus from making a buck to serving my audience.

What is your favorite way to earn money passively?
I love the non-traditional stuff. Books are fabulous, as are pay-per-click columns and affiliate links, but my bootcamp by far is the most fun and interesting method so far. I am able to provide something unique to my community and can help them far more than I could through another medium. Doing my own audiobooks for *The Bite-Sized Entrepreneur* series would be a close second, as it is also different and more intimate than other approaches.

What is the most surprising source of your passive income?
The bootcamp. I asked my email list community how I could serve them best. The biggest request was for the bootcamp. I had it up and running within a week, and we were off to the races. It was a great experience.

What are the most overlooked sources of passive income for writers?
Diversifying what they've already done. For instance, if your beat is profiling CEOs for business magazines, then you could package the unedited interviews into a book and publish it yourself, or teach a course on becoming a master interviewer, or consult organizations on what traits successful business leaders have in common.

What is the one thing writers new to passive income should know?
It's not as complex as it seems. In fact, it will eventually take less work than doing the daily grind. You deserve to be paid continually for your contribution, not just a one-time check.

Writing *The Bite-Sized Entrepreneur* trilogy has been a wonderful, challenging road! There are countless people who have been supportive along the way.

YOUR NEXT STEPS

Are you ready to make your passive income path? Or have these techniques made an impact on your career? We'd love to hear from you! Reach out at damon@damonbrown.net / jeanettehurt@sbcglobal.net or connect on Twitter at @browndamon/@byjeanettehurt and let us know your feedback.

Here are some next steps to make your best passive income opportunities happen.

HAVE DAMON & JEANETTE SPEAK ON THE BUSINESS OF WRITING
http://www.damonbrown.net / http://www.jeanettehurt.com

Damon and Jeanette would love to hear about your events for writers. As veteran freelance journalists, authors, and speakers, Damon and Jeanette specialize in the business of writing. They have keynoted events with American Society of Journalists and Authors, Kohler Wisconsin, American University, Wisconsin Writers Association, and other organizations, and have spoken together dozens of times.

Do Damon's the Bite-Sized Entrepreneur Boot Camp

http://www.bsbootcamp.com

This six-part, self-guided course will bring the best out of your current productivity, focus, and creativity. Taking the best-selling book series a step further, THE BITE-SIZED ENTREPRENEUR boot camp is perfect to do at your own pace with my guidance through video, audio, and text. Join through JoinDamon.me to get a special discount on the course and even some one-on-one coaching opportunities!

http://www.JoinDamon.me

Get your free BITE-SIZED ENTREPRENEUR toolkit to gain even more insight into your next steps. You'll also get exclusive content, early previews of new goodies, and more!

WORK WITH JEANETTE

http://www.jeanettehurt.com

Let's chat about your needs, especially for speaking and instructing on culinary and drink topics. As the author of nine culinary and drink books, with two more in the pipeline, I've taught classes on cocktail history, cocktail making, tapas, dehydrating foods, cheese and beverage pairing, and so much more. I've also consulted to develop pairings menus for cocktails, cheese, tea, and more. I'm also available for writing, editing, recipe development, and ghostwriting.

ACKNOWLEDGEMENTS

Thank you to cover artist Bec Loss as well as Andrea King Collier, Kelly K. James, and Rochelle Melander for sharing their passive income experiences. Appreciation for The American Society of Journalists and Authors for being an endless wealth of knowledge and sponsoring our "Make Money in Your Sleep" panel that inspired the book.

And love to Kyle & Quinn, and Parul, Alec & Abhi, for their love.

ABOUT THE AUTHORS

Damon Brown is a long-time journalist and author of several books, most notably *Our Virtual Shadow: Why We Are Obsessed with Documenting Our Lives Online* (TED Books 2013) and *Porn & Pong: How Grand Theft Auto, Tomb Raider and Other Sexy Games Changed Our Culture* (Feral House 2008), as well as his newest book, *Bring Your Worth: Level Up Your Creative Power, Value & Service to the World* (Self-published 2019). THE PASSIVE WRITER is his 22nd book.

Damon co-founded the social meetup app Cuddlr while being the primary caretaker to his infant son. It went number one on the Apple App store twice, changing the cultural conversation around platonic intimacy. The app was acquired less than a year after it launched, and the whirlwind experience inspired Damon's popular *Inc.com* column Sane Success as well as *The Bite-Sized Entrepreneur*.

You can catch Damon in *Playboy*, *Fast Company*, and *Entrepreneur*, as well as at any locale that serves really spicy food. He lives in Las Vegas,

Nevada, with his wife, two young sons, and bottles of hot sauce.

Connect with him at www.JoinDamon.me or on Twitter at @browndamon.

Jeanette Hurt is the award-winning writer and author of nine culinary and drink books, including Seal Press's critically acclaimed *Drink Like a Woman*. THE PASSIVE WRITER is her 10th book. Currently, she is writing her eleventh and twelfth books: *The Cider Rules* for Skyhorse Publishing and *The Wisconsin Cocktail Book* for the University of Wisconsin Press. She also has penned *The Cheeses of California: A Culinary Travel Guide*, which received the 2010 Mark Twain Award for Best Travel Book, *The Cheeses of Wisconsin: A Culinary Travel Guide*, which also received Mark Twain recognition, and *The Complete Idiot's Guide to Wine and Food Pairing*. As a full-time journalist, Jeanette has written about spirits, wine, and food for SuperCall.com, TalesoftheCocktail.com, TheKitchn.com, *The Four Seasons Magazine*, *Wine Enthusiast*, *Gourmet, Saveur, HOTELS Magazine, Milwaukee Home, Milwaukee Magazine*, Entrepreneur.com, Esquire.com, and dozens more publications, including several in-flight magazines. She is in development talks with a major publisher to become a regular columnist. Jeanette is a regular correspondent about beverages and food for NPR Affiliate WUWM's *Lake Effect,* and she has appeared on several television and radio shows, including the Martha Stewart Living Radio to discuss food and spirits. She is a regular recipe developer of both cocktails and food for several different publications and companies, and she is passionate about all things food and drink.

Over the course of her career, she's interviewed more than 100 spirits professionals, bartenders, brewers, winemakers, and bar historians, and she's been a featured speaker and instructor at the Kohler Food and Wine Experience, The Big Cheese at the Osthoff Resort, the American Society of Journalists and Authors, Wine and Dine Wisconsin, Drink Like a Woman Bike and Drink event in Missouri Wine Country, and the Wisconsin Writers Association. When she's not writing, traveling, cooking or shaking up some concoction, she can usually be found walking along Milwaukee's lakefront with her husband, their son, and their new puppy.

Connect with her on Twitter and Instagram at @ByJeanetteHurt or through her website, www.jeanettehurt.com.

www.ingramcontent.com/pod-product-compliance
Lightning Source LLC
Chambersburg PA
CBHW071215220526
45468CB00002B/611